Worship Worthy

Alliterative Adoration

By Timothy M. Shorey

Worship Worthy
Alliterative Adoration

To my dear wife with whom I have grown to love Jesus more every day.

Together we have found that he is more than wonderful, more than words can tell, more than enough, more than life itself.

INTRODUCTION

This devotional came about almost by accident. It started with a simple posting on my Facebook page in which I strung a few "A" words together that unexpectedly had invaded my devotional time—words adoring the wonder and beauty of my Savior. The next morning it occurred to me to try "B" and it developed from there into a 26 day journey into joy and worship.

Being a preacher I have often found alliteration a helpful tool in teaching, an ancient poetic device aimed to create beauty in the soul and a kind of idea-stickiness for the mind. I'll never forget laughing out loud while reading a fairly meaty book on theology. The author, having paraded a panoply of penned "P" points paused parenthetically to plead: "a preacher's ploy or pointedness. Pardonable? Perhaps" (J.I. Packer). This piece of Packerian playfulness prompted pleasure. It also reminded me that alliteration doesn't have to be cheesy. It is often helpful, and it can be beautiful. Whether or not *Worship Worthy* is either will be up to others to decide. But I do know this: in this flight into words I have seen my Savior afresh, and I am glad.

My inspiration for *Worship Worthy: Alliterative Adoration* is drawn from three sources. It begins with a winsome model. Psalm 119 is a marvelous piece of alliterative poetry. There are twenty-two sections in the Psalm, corresponding to the number of letters in the Hebrew alphabet in which it was originally written. Each section is headed by a succeeding letter of the alphabet, and, to top it off, each verse in each section begins with that letter of the Hebrew alphabet. This shows us that whether for beauty's sake alone, or as a memory aid (the motive is likely both), alliteration is a winsome divinely-inspired, God-sanctioned artistic teaching device.

Besides this winsome model I have also been affected by a wondrous title. Jesus is called "the Alpha and Omega" (Revelation 1:8). These are the Greek letters equivalent to our "A" and "Z". Jesus is where it begins and where it ends. This wonderful title declares the stunning theological truth that Jesus is sovereign over history, and the cause and climax of it all. This became my motivation to adore from A to Z.

And finally, my inspiration derives from a wonderful Person. Once my heart was taken up into the duo-theme of the Person and Work of Christ, I did not want to stop. When "Z" arrived my heart sank. But then it occurred to me to turn my rather hastily crafted Facebook entries into something more substantial and enduring. What you hold in your hands is the result.

Whether or not you find the style winsome, I dearly hope you find the Subject wonderful. My prayer is that you will catch a fresh focused glimpse of the glory and beauty of Jesus. And I hope that having seen him again you will love him all the more until to meet him, your spirit soars. In the end this is not a preacher's ploy for pointedness. It is a lover's lisp, a saved sinner's stutter, a pardoned prodigal's poor praise; yes, a slave-turned-son's stammering song sung to his Savior. Perhaps it will give voice to your heart too.

Ancient of Days. Above all.
Alone in Three.
All-knowing. All-seeing. All around.
August. Awesome. Adonai.
Alpha. At the beginning Already was.

Ark of Safety. Ark of the Covenant. Adam the Second.
Archetype of All. Apostle of our Confession.

Alive in Mary's womb. Announced by angel song.
Affirmed by wonders great. Attacked by senseless hate.
Anguished, sweating blood. Appalled to drink the cup.
Arrested in the garden. Abandoned by his friends.
Accused by evil liars. Assaulted by the soldiers.
Affixed upon a cross.
Accounted as a sinner. Accursed by God above.
Alone in the abyss.
Atoning for our sins. Appeasing of God's wrath.

Arisen from the dead.

Affirmed by empty tomb. Ascended through the clouds.
Ascribed as Lord of All.

Acquitting through his righteousness.
Appealing aid for all. Amazing in his grace.
Attentive to his Church.
Abiding in our hearts. Advising by his Word.
Available in trial. Abounding in his love.

Acclaimed in every tongue. Awaited by his Bride.
Appointed for a Day. Appearing in the sky.
Astonishing to see.
Alarming all his foes. Avenging all his saints.

Adorning all his own. Adored by earth and heaven.
All in All to All.
Amen and Amen.

Being, not becoming. Begotten, not made.
Beloved by God the Father.

Before the beginning. Beyond time.
Boundless Deity. Blazing Light.
Blessed by angels. Burning Bush. Branch of Jesse.

By the Father's side. By the Father sent.
Born in Bethlehem. Born to die. Best Man ever. Blameless Lamb.
Betrayed. Blamed. Besieged. Bruised. Battered. Broken. Buried.

Back.

Borne on clouds. Been exalted. Bestowed a Name.

Bread of Heaven. Breastplate of Righteousness. Bond of Peace.
Beacon of Light. Bastion of Mercy.

Blessed Redeemer. Bold intercessor. Banner before us.

Bellwether for the blinded.
Bulwark for the besieged.
Big Brother for the bullied.
Bearer for the burdened.
Balm for the blistered.
Bridegroom for the bypassed.
Benediction for the beleaguered.

Beggars' Bounty. Believers' Boast.

Before. Behind. Beneath.

Better.
Better than the old.
Better Nature. Better Name. Better Office.
Better Priesthood. Better Sacrifice. Better Holy Place.
Better Covenant. Better Promises. Better Hope.
Better City. Better Country. Better Rest.

Beheld.
Bane to evildoers. Brandishing Warrior.
Bloody-robed. Banishing Judge.

Beheld.
Beloved to all believers. Beaming Bridegroom.
Bright Sun. Beautiful Savior.

Beatific Vision.
Blessedness evermore.

Cause. Creator.
Cosmic King. Canticle of angels.
Covenanter of Grace.
Called by the Father.

Canaan's Fulfillment. Consolation of Israel.

Conceived by the Holy Spirit.
Carried by Mary.
Cradled with cattle. Child given.

Come.
Come to do his Father's will.
Come to seek the lost.
Come to save sinners.
Come to call to repentance.
Come to preach good news.
Come to give us abundant life.

Circumcised under Law.
Clothed in humility.
Compassionate Healer.
Consecrated sacrifice.

Cast off. Condemned. Crucified Creator. Crimson Cross.
Curse-bearer. Crushed by God.
Covenant-sealer.

Carried from the cross that bore him
Closed within a stone-cold tomb
Cast into the depths before him
Contended with the powers of doom
Crushed the serpent's raging head
Conquering Death, its fear to ban
Captives freed, on high he led
Claimed the spoils, gave gifts to man.

Christ the Prophet. Christ the Priest. Christ the King.

Covering for our sins. Chastisement for our peace.
Cleansing for our conscience.

Conduit of grace.
Counselor. Comfort. Constant. Committed.
Carrier. Completer.

Coming.
Commander of the Lord's hosts.
Caesar's Lord.
Condemning Judge.
Consuming Fire.

Creation's Cleanser.
Cornerstone.
Climax.
Compelling vision.
Celebration.

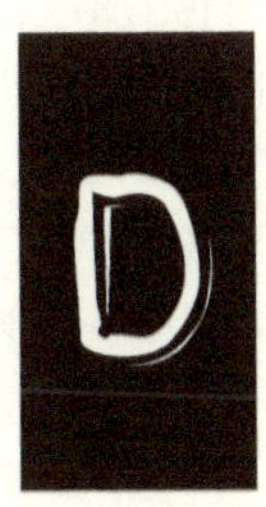

Deity unDiluted, unDivided, unDiminished, unDerived.
Daybreak of Creation. Dawn of Time. Dwarfing all.

Doxology of the seraphim.
Desire of the Nations.

Due.

Dayspring from on high.
Delivered by Mary. David's Son. David's Lord.
Deity down here.
Doer of good.
Demon-banisher. Disease-healer. Despair-releaser.
Darkness-dispeller. Decay-reverser.

Denied by Peter. Deserted by friends. Disobeyed by all.
Despised. Disowned. Defamed. Disdained. Displayed.
Delivered to die. Descent.

Determined before time.
Damned by God.
Drank the dregs.
Dead.

Day of Atonement. Debt-Payer. Damnation-Deliverer.

Dead no more.
Death-killer. Dragon-slayer.

Doubted by Didymus.
Demonstrated alive.
Drawn into the heavens.
Dominion as Lord.
Declared to the nations.
Defeating his enemies.
Dread of the wicked.
Depth of mercy.
Deposit of grace.

Defender of the chosen few
Daily grace like morning dew
Dear, devoted, dying Friend
Dwelling in us to the end.

Due again.

Dominus Christus.
Doorway to Heaven.
Daybreak of eternity.
Dazzling in beauty.
Dancing in joy.
Deep, deep love.
Dreams discovered.
Desire deeply drunk.
Delight defying description.
Days without end.

Eternally Equal with the Father.
Exact Image of God.
El Shaddai.

Eden's Host. Eve's promised seed. Exodus from Egypt.
Eshcol's Valley. Ebal's curse-bearer.

Equality not grasped. Enormity Emptied. Elegance Enveiled. Effulgence
Eclipsed.
Enters a womb. Embodies deity.
Escapes Ephrata.
Eschews Satan's enticements.
Embraces sinners.

Encounters evil men.
Endures hell's worst. Empties wrath's Cup.
Erases our debt. Earns our everything.

Eludes decay. Escapes the grave.
Enters the Holy Place. Entreats the Father.
Ensures needed grace. Encourages the weary.
Eases the burdened. Emancipates the bound.

Enthroned.

Enlists his church. Entrusts his truth.
Envisions our faith. Equips our hand.
Employs our gifts. Establishes our work.
Extends our sufferings. Enlivens our endurance.
Encircles our camp. Envelops our hearts.
Enables our success. Enlarges our borders.
Expands his kingdom.

Ever-good. Ever-faithful. Ever-true.
Ever-living. Everlasting.

Eternity's Entrance and Essence:
Evaluates our works, Effuses his praise, Elevates our place,
Enthralls our spirits, Elicits our adoration, and
Enjoys it all.

From forever Godhead true
Father, Spirit, One with you.
Flying seraphs "Holy" cry
Fairest Lord, enthroned on high.

Foreshadowed in the lamb and blood,
Famous ark that rode the flood.
Fashioned tabernacle too,
Foretold the work you came to do.

Form of God, you did not cling
Forsook the glory, emptying.
Form of slave, redemption planned
Found in likeness as a man.
Fasting in the wilderness –
Facing every hellish test –
Fitting you, my soul to bless, to
Feel the pain of my distress.

Fully obeyed the Father's will
Faced the Cross, accurse´d kill.
Filthy sin in blackened hue
Fault in me, fixed on you.
Forsaken by your Father there
Facing wrath, my griefs to bear.

Five bleeding wounds you bore for me
Fragrant incense, Calvary.
Fully absolved through these I am
Friend of sinners, foreknown Lamb.
For the debt my sins decreed
Finished payment, guilty freed.

From the dead you rose up then
Fact of hist'ry proved to men.
Father-lifted, glory given
Foremost Name on earth, in heaven.
First in rank, preeminent
From there, to here, and back were sent.

Firm Foundation, Fortress high
Find and bind me or I die.
Flowing river, Fountain spring
Forgive and wash the sins I bring.

Freedom Fighter fierce for me
(Foes repent, or footstool be).
Fealty deep I owe to you
Friend and Brother, love is due.
Fame and faith, may they be found
Far and wide, your glory's crown.

Founder, Finisher, and Feast
Freely offered me, the least
From your fullness fill with grace
Forever favor, face to face.

God
Glo**ri**a
Grand**e**ur
Gl**a**dness
Girded with **St**rength

Glor**i**ous
Genesi**s**

Guil**t**less
Golgot**ha**
Gav**e** himself

Gui**L**t-releasing
G**o**spel-singing
G**ra**ce-gripping
Guar**d**ing, Girding

Good
Good Shephe**r**d
Gath**e**rer
Gr**a**nite foundation
Guidepos**t**
Gent**l**y leads
Guileless**l**y loves

Gif**t** and Giver
Gr**oo**m of heaven

Gibbet of **b**lood
Garm**e**nt of Righteousness

Gone to Pre**p**are
Going to **r**eturn
G**a**teway to Glory
Govern**i**ng King
Glorifie**s** us
Gold**e**n Throne
Guarantee**d**

Habitant of Eternity. Here before the Hills.
Holy. Holy. Holy.
His Highness. His Holiness. His Honor.
Happy in Himself. Having no need. His Father's Heart.

Heard at Creation. Holds it together.

Hung the moon in place.
Hurled the stars in space.
Has planet orbits traced.
Harnessed by his embrace.

Hated by heaven's highest angel. Heart-broken by human hubris.

His heel hell will crush
Hell's head he will crush.

Harbinger of Hope. Heir of David's throne
Heralded by heavenly hosts. Held in Virgin's heart. Human.
Hungered like us. Handled hell's worst.

Helped the helpless.
Healed the hurting.
Hove out the hellish.
Harangued the hypocrites.
Heart-mourned the hardened.
Hugged the harlots and hated.

Hailed one week. Hissed at the next.
Hosannaed with palms. Hung by nails.
Hated, Harassed, Hunted, and Hanged Hero.

Humans scoff. Hell scorns.
Heaven scowls. He screams.
High noon short-circuits.

History's Hinge.

Hailed alive. Highly exalted. Head of all. Holds Hades' Key.

Highest Heights.
Helmet of Hope. Helmet of Salvation.
Highway to Heaven.

Here for us:
Hearer. Helper. Holder. Healer.

Hope for us:
Harbor. Haven. Heaven. Home.

Happiness.

Hosanna in the Highest.
Hails and Hallelujahs!

I Am:
The One who simply is, and is–
Infinite:
Immeasurable in being and unbounded by space and time; eternally–
Irreducible:
Complete, unchanging, undiminishing, unshrinking Deity; the–
Imago Dei:
God shining forth, the perfect radiance of the Father; long–
Invisible:
Forever unseen; inhabiting–
Inaccessible Light:
A luminous, unapproachable blaze; who became–

Incarnate:
Truly human, God in a body; the–
Ideal Man:
Man as Man was meant to be, truly–
Innocent:
Blameless in the face of full, furious, flaming temptation, the–
Impeccable:
Flawless in holiness, a Paragon of virtue; yet–

Insulted and Impugned:
An intolerable Light in a dark world, hated, slandered, and-
Impaled:
Pierced through hands, feet and side, then left to die; a sacrifice-
Imputed as guilty:
By mutual consent with the Father, bearing our shame, our sins counted
as his; the-
Isolated:
Truly alone—hated by humans, assailed by hell, forsaken by Heaven; then

Interred:
In the tomb; then raised—

Incorruptible:
He whom death could not hold and decay could not touch arose –
Invincible:
Crushing the hosts of hell and the power of Death; a fact-
Indisputable:
By which he is declared Lord over all, and after which the Father crowned
him the –
Inaugurated:
The reigning King on high, with all authority in heaven and earth, exalted
to be-
Intercessor:
The One who prays and pleads in behalf of all he loves and he becomes
for them-

Initiator, Illuminator, Inviter, and Indweller:
He who moves toward, invites in, and dwells with and in all who hear his
voice, shining the light of his grace upon them; forever the-
Inseparable:
Not ever to leave them, no matter what; from whose love they can never
be severed; the-
Immutable:
The same in his love, being and offices yesterday, today, and forever; and
so is-
Inestimable:
He whose worth can never be measured, whose preciousness cannot be
expressed; the-

Invoked:

Whose Bride cries incessantly, "Come Lord Jesus!" in love ever growing and never ceasing; full of hope that he is the–

Imminent:

One who suddenly will part the clouds, riding the stallion to put all things right; and then will be–

Invisible no more:

The Husband-God whom we will see, worship and adore for endless ages; he who will be the end of all our purest longings; the ravishment of all our holy desires. Amen.

Jehovah: Archaic form of YAH, I Am;
Justice-Appeaser: Absorbed God's wrath, vicarious Lamb.

Just: He will do right, that much is sure;
Jealous: His love's great zeal to keep us pure.

Jesus: He saves his people from their sin;
Judgment-Bearer: And took the blame for the mess we're in.

Jehovah-Jireh: 'The Lord provides' is what this meant;
Justification: Treats us as if we're innocent.

Judah's Scepter: The symbol of our Sovereign King;
Joined: In him, God gives us everything.

Judge: He'll wield a final, fearsome rod;
Jacob's Ladder: He leads from earth right up to God.

Jubilant: The overflow of God most blessed;
Joy-giving: To gladden us with all that's best.

Jesu: Purest joy of man's desiring;
Jewel: Treasured pearl our love inspiring.

Journeyed: From heaven to earth and back again;
Jolt: What most will feel at his descent.

Jubilee: Released to endless freedom years;
Joyous: The Face we'll see through grateful tears.

Keystone: the center, locking cosmic core.
Knowledge: of everything from long before.
Knower: of those he chose in ages yore.
Kenosis: stripped off the glory that he wore.
Kid: boy newly born on stable floor.
Kinsman: to cheat and thief and weeping whore.
Knifed: betrayed by Judas—o deplore!
Killed: hanged in shame and bloodied gore.
Kinsman Redeemer: to free the captive, wretched poor.
Kept: from death's decay before day four.
Knocks: to enter hearts, their love implore.
Known: his voice, by those he's calling for.
King of Righteousness: in which we stand, to heaven soar.
Kindness: from endless riches does he pour.
Kingdom-Builder: his whole creation to restore.
Keeper: to bring us safe to heaven's shore.
Keeps: inheritance, for us in store.
King: Judah's Lion set to roar.
Key of Death: unlocking Hades' Death-sealed door.
King of kings: let kings their trembling fears outpour.
Kiss of Peace: he'll put an end to rage and war.
Kingmaker: exalting us from last to fore.
Key: to life with him forevermore.
King of Glory: o come you faithful, and adore!

Light.
Love.

Loved by God.
Lord of Creation.

Lucifer's Envy.

Looked for.
Love's Gift.
Lowly Child.
Light of Men.

Loved by humans.
Laser Words.
Loathed by humans.
Lacerated.
Lanced.
Laid Out.
Lowest parts of the earth.

Lamb slain from before time.
Lamb of God to take away the sin of the world.

Living.
Last Adam.
Lord of Life.
Light of the World.
Ladder.

Lamp for our Feet.
Liberator.
Leader.
Listener.
Longed for.

Lightning Flashing.
Lo! He comes on clouds descending.
Lily of the Valley.
Lustrous.
Luminous.
Lion of the Tribe of Judah.
Lord of lords.
Light of lights.

Leaping, Laughing Lover of My Soul.

Lauded.
Loved.
Lasting.
Last.

Messiah Pre-history

> Mighty God. Most High.
> Monogenes (uniquely begotten), not Made
> Mystererium Tremendum

Messiah Pre-figured

> Melchizedek's Order: a priest with no beginning, end;
> Meshach's Companion: in the furnace to defend;
> Moses' Rock: for water fresh in wilderness;
> Mercy Seat: where Yahweh's grace and glory kiss;
> Mount Moriah: a hill and Lamb he will provide;
> Moving Tabernacle: where we go, he will reside;
> Morning Manna: bread to feed us every day;
> Most Holy Place: by his blood he makes a way.

Messiah Presented

> Mary's Son. Mary's Savior. Mary's Lord. Manger born.
> Man. Matches man, minus misdeeds.
> Miracle worker. Mercy ministry. Message from God.
> Man of Sorrows. Malevolent mob. Mangled flesh. Murdered man.
> Meant to happen.
> Meritorious for us.

Messiah Present

> Messiah is risen. Morning dawns.
> Majesty on High. Mediator of a New Covenant.
>
> Mount Moriah's Meaning. Mount Sinai's Measure.
> Mount Ebal's Mediator. Mount Gerizim's Merit.
> Mount Calvary's Mercy. Mount Zion's Morning.

Master. Motive. Model. Measure. Meaning. Message.
Might. Mainstream. Mainstay. Mountain Mover.

Messiah Preeminent

Morning Star. Marvelous Sight. Majestic scene. Monarch's
scepter.

Mourning's Mute. Music's Melody.
Mine.

Never not.
No sin. No darkness at all.
No bounds.

Night-angel's Noel.
Notorious family tree.
Newborn Son.
Nazareth Carpenter.

Neighbor love not appreciated.
Not known.
Neglected Messiah.
Naked. Nailed. Night-swallowed.

Nullifier of the Laws demands.
Nothing but the Blood.

Night-Scatterer.
Name above all names.
New Day. Noon Day.
North Star. Never-fading Nova.
Now.

Needed. Nourishment. Nurture. New wine.

Near. Never-napping.

Noah's new ark. Naaman's new skin.
Naomi's new hope. Nicodemus' new birth.

No other saving name under heaven.

None else beside, whose-
Name now is, never was not, and never
will not be. Amen.

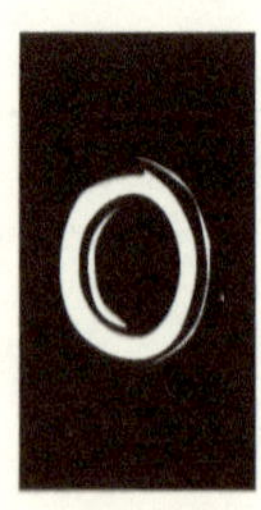

Of the Father's Love: in eternity Begotten;
Only: Son of God, at the Father's side;
Other: the realm his glory must be sought in—
Where mortal man cannot reside.

Omnipotent. Omniscient.
Omnipresent. Omni-competent.

Origin: through him all things that are were made;
Owner: the earth is his and all the skies;
Over all: in heaven his glory is displayed;
On fire: so bright, the angels cover eyes.

Ordained: Prophet-King, by God anointed;
Order of Melchizedek: eternal Priesthood, God-decreed;
Of a Virgin: in purity he was appointed;
Of the Spirit: spared the stain of Adam's seed.

On earth: Galactic Lord, he walked on earth;
One of us: immortal in the realm of man;
Observed the Law: a Righteous One to death, from birth;
Obeyed: surrendered to the Father's plan.

Opposed: Resisted by the world he made;
Odious: and hated by his very own;
Ostracized: outside the camp reproach was laid;
Offered up: on him, when offered, to atone.

Once for all: His sacrifice sufficed for all;
Obtains: the price to purchase us for God;
Offers forgiveness: to promise pardon when we call;
Oath: a pledge of mercy sealed with blood.

Overcame the lure of sin,
Overwhelmed the powers of hell,
Overthrew the grave was in,
Oversees so all is well.

Oppresses: He strikes us down, afflicts the soul;
Opens wounds: He tears us as with Lion's claw;
Offers healing: Then heals and mends to make us whole;
O Lord come: Return o Lord with morning dawn.

On time. Ongoing. Onward.
On the throne. On our side.
On the move. On the way.

Opens heaven.

Only Lord and Master, he
Only God, Our Savior, be.

Ocean-deep love.

Omega.

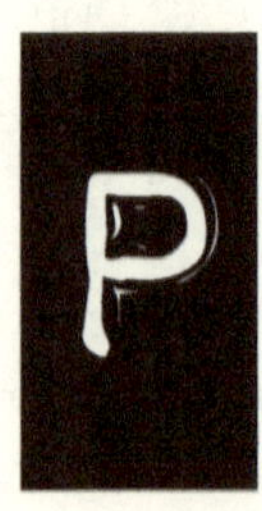

Pre-existent God.
Powerful Creator.
Precious Son.
Point of Origin.
Possessor of All.

Prefigured. Prophesied. Predicted.

Proceeding from eternity.
Placed in a womb.
Pleasing to the Father.
Pierced upon a cross.

Passion consumed.
Poured out.
Propitiating.

Pummeled death to death.
Passed through the heavens.
Preeminent over all.
Prince of Peace.

Prophet: speaking to us infallibly about God.
Priest: bringing us acceptably to God.
Potentate: ruling us authoritatively for God.

Pursuing. Possessing. Praying. Pleading.
Preserving. Providing. Protecting. Purifying.

Pleased. Pleasant. Pleasing.
Personal.
Priceless. Pearl.

Promised.
Preparing a Place.
Planning to return.

Parousia.
Perfection.
Permanent.

Pleasures forevermore.

Quiddity of Life.

Quintessential.
Quintessential Love.
Quintessential Goodness.
Quintessential Beauty.
Quintessential Truth.
Quintessential Man.

Quit on by man.

Quickened from the dead.
Quickener of the dead.

Qualified and Qualifier before God.

Quietus for our debt.
Quieting of our guilt.
Quietness in our storms.

Quencher of thirst.

Quickly coming.

Quest for time and eternity.

Radiance: God's refulgent beauteous rays;
Ruler: Sovereign One, from ancient days;
Reason: Cosmic cause of all that is;
Real: Being, essence, fullness, his.

Reigning: From highest throne, does as he wills;
Regal: Majestic train his temple fills;
Righteous: Unstained by neither sin nor wrong;
Resplendent: Ceaseless theme of seraph song.

Relinquished: Exchanged his throne for cattle stall;
Reveals: The Face of God unveiling all;
Resolved: In love unflinching, suffered loss;
Rejected: All-forsaken on the Cross.

Redeemer: Set us free through ransom blood;
Reconciler: To reunite our souls to God;
Risen: Raised again, Death's fear has banned;
Right Hand: Sits as Lord at God's right hand.

Rebirth: His Spirit does the dead infuse;
Renewal: His daily grace the heart renews;
Restoration: Restores the years once locust-eaten;
Revival: Lifts up the weary and down-beaten.

Refuge: Around to shelter in the storm;
Rear Guard: Behind to shield and watch and warn;
Rock: Beneath to be our footing sure;
Rock of Ages: In cleft of which we hide secure.

Romancer: Jesus, Lover of my soul;
Rest: Where broken, weary hearts are whole;
Refrain: Eternal hymn the saints are voicing;
River: Rushing river of rejoicing.

Rightness: Essential rightness is in him;
Reality: True Truth, transcending human whim;
Reason: Because he is, and marches on;
Rubicon: He has become our Rubicon.

Returning: He will return to make things right;
Rider: Astride a stallion, stunning white;
Recompense: A bloodied sword shall recompense;
Reason to Fear: Trembling sinners, no defense.

Resurrection: The saints shall hear his voice and rise;
Reward: To hear "Well done" with tear-filled eyes;
Re-Creation: Behold all things shall be made new;
Re-assurance: All these words are Faithful, True.

Solitary.
Self-existent.
Self-sufficient.
Sovereign.
Shrouded in beginning-lessness.

Sunrise.
Sun of Righteousness.
Shining Light.
Source of All.

Shadows.
Subject of Prophecy.
Star of Jacob.
Scepter of Israel.
Sacrificial Lambs.
Shekinah Glory.

Son of God. Son of Man. Son of David. Son of Mary.

Spared not. Suffering Servant of Yahweh.

Spurned.
Slandered.
Silent Lamb.
Struck.
Scorned.
Stripped.
Surrounded by lions.
Sneered at.
Stabbed.
Slain.

Surrenders his spirit.

Sacrifice. Sin-Bearer. Substitutionary Atonement.
Sweet aroma before God.
Sinners' Surety.
Sundered Sanctuary Veil.

Silence.
Silence sustained.
Silence still.

Shout!
Shatters death's chain.
Sheol-escaping.
Serpent-crushing.
Satan-binding.

Sovereign.
Seeker.
Savior.
Shepherd.

Support. Succor. Sustenance. Strength.
Safety. Shield. Shade.
Steadfast Love.

Searcher and Sentencer of senseless sinners.

Seen by saints.

Soul-Satisfier.
Sorrow-Eraser.
Salvation-Bringer.

Singer. Songwriter. Song.

Selah.

There.
True God.
Thrice holy. Temple glory.
Torah-Giver.

Transcendent over time, territory, treason,
terrorists, trends, troubles and tears.

True Man.
Tabernacle of God.
Teacher. Truth.
Toucher of the untouchables.

Totally tempted, yet true.
Turned against. Tried. Thorn-crowned. Tree-cursed.
Tomb-laid.

Tomb-busting. Triumphant. Throne-exalted.

Truce with God for us. Total access for us to God.

Today.

Tender. Trustworthy. Timely. True.
Tear-sympathizer. Trial-carrier. Tumult-Tamer.
Tear-drier. Tapestry-weaver.

Turning point. Transformation. True north.

Trumpet announced.

Tribunal. Touchstone. Tester and Trier of all.
Terror to the treacherous.
Tower to the trusting.

Tomorrow's Dawn. Tree of Life. Table-preparer.
Truth.
Timeless Treasure.

Unmoved Mover. Unmade Maker.
Undivided Deity. Unapproachable Light.

Upright. Untaught. Unequalled. Unchanging.
Unfazed. Ubiquitous. Unbounded. Unlike us.

Unselfish. Uniquely born. Us-like.
Unleavened. Unimpeachable. Unblemished.

Unknown. Unsought. Unloved. Undressed.
Unguarded. Unleashed Upon. Utterly forsaken.
Unjustly killed. Underground.

Undead.

Us-ward.
Union with Him. Uniting to God.

Upholding. Uplifting. Unhasting. Unwasting.
Unfailing. Unwavering.

Understanding. Undergirding.
Underneath (and all around).
Unction.

Universal Lord. Unrivaled King. Unassailable Fortress.

Upward calling, highest prize
Unveiled beauty, ravished eyes
Unending bliss, the offspring of—
Unhindered, undiminished Love
Ultimate: this Lord and King
Ultimate in everything.

Very God of Very God.
Very Man of Very Man.

Vast. Venerable Ancient of Days. Virtuous.
Voice of Creation. Voice of Reason. Voice of God.

Virgin born. Veiled in flesh. Visitation from on high.

Viciously Violated. Verily Vindicated.
Voluntary Victim. Vanquishing Victor.
Vicarious Sacrifice. Vestment of righteousness. Veil-Render.

Valiant Lover. Validated Lord.

Valued. Veracity.
Vitality. Vigor. Vital. Vine. Vinedresser.
Visitor in our Valleys. Valley-Leveler.

Vested with all Authority.
Volcano of wrath. Vault of mercy.
Vengeance-robed. Victims' Vindicator.

Vanguard of heaven.
Visible Vivid Verity.

Vivifying Vision.

Without Beginning.
Who Was and Will Be.
Wondrous. Wisdom. World-Creator.
Worshiped by Winged Seraphs.

Word of God. Word with God.
Word Who Was and is God.

Woman-borne. Womb-delivered.
Word made flesh. Word with us.

Wonder-Worker. Wandering Rabbi. Wonderful Counselor.
World-forsaken. Willing Sacrifice. Wounded God.

Woken from the dead.
Worthy Lamb. Wonderful Lion. Warrior Lord.

Wherever We Walk. Whenever We Weep. Why We Worship.

Winepress for the wicked.
Warning for the wayward.
Way for the wandering.
Welcome for the waylaid.
Wakening for the wasted.
Wisdom for the witless.
Washing for the willing.
Wealth for the wanting.
Wellness for the wounded.
Wonder for the wretched.
Wind-breeze for the wilted.

Wellspring for the weak.
Water for the worn.
Wine for the weeping.
Wings for the weary.

Waited for. Worth the Wait.

Wedding Host. Wed to us.

Worship Worthy.
Wondrous sight.
Without end.

Existent in himself.
Expressly in God's Image.
Exact in knowledge.
Exquisite in holiness.
Excelling in virtue.
Exceeding in beauty.
Extraordinary in everything.

Exerter in Creation.

Exposited in Scripture.

Exposed in Incarnation.
Experienced in temptation.
Exemplary in obedience.
Extreme in sacrifice.
Executed in darkness.
Exiled in dereliction.

Expiatory in crucifixion.
Exonerated in resurrection.
Exalted in ascension.
Excellent in ascription.

Exonerator in grace.
Expressive in affection.
Expedient in providence.
Exorbitant in kindness.
Exhorter in care.
Existing in us.
Existential in reality.

Examiner in truth.
Exhaustive in review.
Exacting in justice.
Executor in judgment.
Exclusive in mercy.
Expelling in wrath.

Expected in the morning.
Expulsive in triumph.
Exuberant in love.
Excited in his marriage.
Exultant in joy.
Extravagant in heaven.
Extolled in eternity.

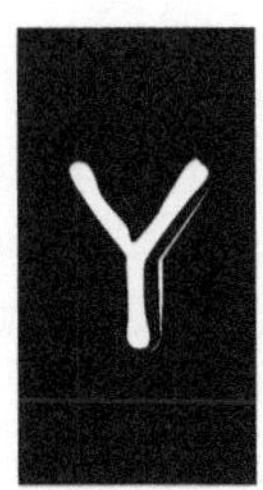

Yahweh, by ancient names long known:
Yahweh God of gods.
Yahweh God Most High.
Yahweh God of Hosts.
Yahweh Mighty in Battle.
Yahweh God of Truth.
Yahweh God of My Salvation.
Yahweh Will Provide.

Years without beginning. Years without end. Years without number.
Yule-born. Young child. Youth of Nazareth.

Yielded.
Yielded to God Above.
Yielded to mother and father.
Yielded to knife and Law.
Yielded to thugs and thorns.
Yielded to nail and spear.
Yielded to slab and tomb.
Yielded like a lamb.

Yom Kippur

Yet Alive.

Yoke.
Yoke for the weary.
Yoke for the burdened.
Yoke made easy.
Yoke made light.

Yes.
Yes to all our noes.
Yes to all our can'ts.
Yes to all our needs.
Yes to all our hopes.
Yes to all our longings.
Yes to "Will I finish?"
Yes to "Will I survive?"
Yes to "Can I make it?"
Yes to "Does he love me?"
Yes to all God's promises.

Yours.
Your election.
Your propitiation.
Your redemption.
Your justification.
Your reconciliation.
Your adoption.
Your sanctification.
Your glorification.

Your only way to God.
Your only truth about God.
Your only life in God.

Yours...and mine, too.

Yesterday. Yet today. Yes, tomorrow.
Yearned for. Yet to come.

Yahweh Shalom.
Yes and Amen.

Zealous for God. Zealous with God.
Zealous as God.
Zealous for us. Zealous in love.

Zeus', Zoroaster's, Zodiac's, and Zen's demise.

Zebulon's Great Light.
Zechariah (I)'s Cleansing Fountain.
Zacchaeus' Seeking Friend.
Zechariah (II)'s Glorious Sunrise.
Zephaniah's Loving Singer.

Zest for the careworn.
Zeal for the careless.
Zig and Zag for the clichéd.

Zion's Cornerstone is he
Zion's Way he'll ever be
Zion's Temple is our Lord
Zion's Lamp has been restored
Zion's Sun forever shines
Zion's King is Man-Divine
Zion's people, harps unhung—have
Zion's Song upon their tongue
Zion's City, ever his
Zion's Lamb—o worthy is!

Zenith for all eternity.

"Z" itself: the Last and the Goal of all that now is,
ever was, or evermore shall be. Amen.

ABOUT THE AUTHOR

Born of missionary parents Tim spent his early years in Japan. His parents served in missionary and pastoral ministry for more than fifty years, providing a heritage of faith and devotion which he treasures to this day. He was converted at age 15, and has served as a pastor in New Jersey and Pennsylvania from 1982 until now. He also provides care for numerous pastors and churches as the Northeast Regional Leader for Sovereign Grace Churches.

Tim has been married for 36 years to his wife, Gayline. They have six grown children who have provided them with nine grand-children thus far.

Tim may be contacted at tmshorey@gmail.com.